ARTIFICE

LAVINIA SINGER

A THING MADE

Work Study

The work takes her to Amsterdam, LA and Seoul.
Or else, it's work in the studio with the old toilet
bowls stuffed with soil and seedlings, cold light
streaks each morning, the school playground
crashing up next door. A recurrent cat. It's true
she works most days, the routine becoming
normality, just work. This: her office, her desk.
Here's the most recent, what she's been working
on for weeks now – months? – existing before it's
itself, bleeding paint. So, how does it work – I
mean, physicalities, substance shift, where daily
work turns to more than just that? The brush pots,
clippings, tinted tea mugs and dead colour worked
into wall creases, packages marked 'sold' stacked
by catalogues webbed in dust; out of, I'd almost
call it junk, the whole works, it is made – the Work.

Annunciation

his name depends
on the smooth
   scratch & burn
  in our hands
his reputation's end
  we pick at the
blanking sheet of wax
    each outline
  etched to
birth
some new
  immaculate form
asleep beneath white
an angel thrusts
  his gift of lilies
blessed virgin
our patron's palace
brocading the window
  all yet buried
  from view
exposure
  dipping & so
     to ink
  impressions
prints upon prints
  disseminated
   black & white
across the globe for
  judgement
we
  within these walls
audience to his original
  the sole work –
strokes & colour-floods
  the ache of paint
  on cloth – of scant
worth
   heirs
  of our labour's hours
the copies will proclaim
him
   the acid bites

The Painting of the Queen

Time touches ev'ry Mortal, be it morphew and wrinckles
or signs of the small Poxe

     The work suffers from abrasion and craquelure
       with a surface of aged fly specks

But with care and by Art
we can make for ourselves another Face

     Evidence of various
       restorative skills and techniques

For cleansing the Skin, anoint with
the oyl of sweet Almonds

     Applied varnish
       and a thermoplastic resin

The Venetian Ceruse whitens
with shine like a Pearl

     Characteristic blanching
       and thick chalking across all

But for stubbournest Markes
employ black patches cut in Starres or half Moons

     The most damaged parts
       are coated in opaque over-paint

Make rubies of the Cheeks with Vermilion
Hair burning yellow with Celandine

     Alongside spreading bloom
       and fugitive pigments

The juice of Belladonna drop'd into the Eyes
gifts a most excellent Sparkle

     Optically, a high specular gloss

And thus the most excellent and glorious Person
a Goulden Phenix reborn

     From this loaded painting
      the original can only be imagined

Wood Cut

It's a gift, this devil
of a subject. Reams
of material, ample
anecdotes. How best
to advertise, to dazzle
with honed craft?
Purges, plundering,
poisoned wells . . .
the basic vocabulary
of villainy. It's the dark
details that truly transfix
– eyes on stalks –
what none would dare
imagine: a skeletal
donkey speared beside
its master, the turbans
of Turkish emissaries
nailed to their temples,
those holy monks who
got to heaven faster,
mothers with babes
in open graves . . .
I know what's at stake.
To bait the buyers,
delineate the art of dying
(there is no good death).
Picture this: a table
laid in bucolic scene,
soft hill curves in mono-
chromatic symphony
meet whipped lines
like thick spines & only
slowly would you start
to recognise wretched
shapes, crooked agonies,
split, pinned in human
palisade, & there he sits,
Son of the Dragon,
in his forest of strange

fruit, regally arrayed,
set-browed with piercing
stare, ready to dip his
bread in that which drips
above his head – yes,
time to cut some wood.

Spar Box

fluorspar, n.
– OED

classical Latin *fluor* wooden box a unique part of our mining heritage
exhibition   medical context morbid discharge flux   tribute to the
craftsmanship peepshow fronted glass   (2nd cent. ad) witherite
a firmament of stars   also   alstonite goethite   menstruation
5th   national collection   crack Augustine   pick + shovel
galena shells   resembling ornate gems   (1546   in Agricola
pyrite siderite sandstone   see   spectacular below
chalcedony sphalerite   containing   crystal grotto   fluorine
1741)   unrivalled splendour   or   smithsonite   German
barytocalcite   earlier   source   multiplying
spathosus   genuine folk art   limonite
admitting of easy cleavage   after   candlelit glows
Flussspat   silver   mirrors   studded   aragonite
(see   zinc   ore   cerussite   -or *suffix*   middle
fantastical scene   low   ornament   heavy as
lead   *sper*   also   Victorian combs.   baryte quartz
sparglas -*kalk*   high   ravine   related to   Old English
diamond   moors   cruel   stone   astonishingly ornate
gypsum   *spærstán*   fissure   and   sparstone
faceted fluorite   obscure   glittering   origins   ankerite
siderite   remote prize apart   dart dispute   steel calcite   mine
hematite vein of rock bandy words arte povera blooded woodwork

Waxworks

human likeness
cast of Adonis
unspotted, golden
so we may mould
according to pleasure
here saved
what else would
be lost, hollowed
feast for the eyes
the sweetest lies
within the strong
– look upon, ye!
brazen celebrity
hot sugar

the rays soften
feathers on waves
impressionistic
a kind of light
writing, real
as a photograph
you may touch
sirens blanked
on the street
O ambition
flaunts this vault
– arrested fame
something
decomposes

the wax, its shape
these candles
wick time
ideal portraits
turned effigies
masks to seal
the faces of the dead
receive, retain
forms of forms
work their way
counterfeit change
– incredible, still
to crave
a clean slate

Portrait in Hex

SKIN

shielded kin
blood beats

sounding, crucible

#FFF5EE

LIPS

promised feast
the thorn's prick

spelling, sweet

#B94E48

EYES

lidded depths
wrecks in the silvering

sighing, acquiesce

#778BA5

HAIR

treasured rays
laid waste

spinning, whirr

#C39953

Architecture

blown away – by the crenellating stone &
vaulting ribcage good gothic windows foil
lacing gold & twisted glass stained glows
in the hush candlelit from an aged
iconography spun through the clerestory
still the columns brag cryptic pediments
O swept awnings the fretwork such august
impress call it *grandeur!* clusters sing
cool worship led in beauty what a species
achieves I desire to hold & capture thus
strange the wish to ingest keep close for
the small most other days all the cold
imperfect when – what we lose blows away

BASELESS
FABRIC

The Mapmaker's Daughter

When the door is shut, I know He's at work.
Creating worlds by the flow of a pen tip –
I used to think He was a god, crafting
with quadrant and accurate vernier.
In seven days separating water from land,
a straining Newton with compasses clutched
dextrously mapping Particles of Light.

When the electricity blared its last,
He took to lighting candle stubs, the flames
licking the ink so the colours blinked like stained glass.
Toffee shores glowed like half-moons, round
with sand tumbling like uncountable kisses.
From coast to peninsula, each scrub and each dab
plotted a country, a nation, a home.

When bored in the house and Him locked away
I'd be content with an old mottled print
scouted out at a car boot sale,
amid chipped teacup and watering can.
A *mappa mundi*, Dad said. No ordinary map!
Its circles and symbols resembled a code,
and the land it outlaid was like none I had known.

When science and story were one,
and the globe some plump orb of possibility,
where cave-dwelling giants mixed with dog-headed men,
dwarves riding on crocodiles and charmers of snakes.
I'd stare at those figures holding their heads
like swollen shopping bags, and little folk
gathering silkworms by the Tree of Life.

When the forests here went, I missed the green
of Dad's work. Colour of the kind that sits
in front of your face, sucking your eyeballs.
The white of the icebergs, too, melted away.
His parchment now looks like something deceased,
brown like tough skin with odd cities freckled,
rivers of wrinkles and washed stains of blue.

O the blue!

Now oceans rise and Neptune conquers all,
the tide a hiccup choking up upon shore.
Nothing can stop the waves, as they soar –
stealing strips of terrain, smashing houses and shops.
Now all that Dad's map shows are disparate islands,
bobbing bits of broken turf, continents cracked.
The monsters have gone now, and many men, too.

Now all Dad needs is tins of cyan,
turquoise and teal and ultramarine,
the blues of midnight, lavender and sky.
And me? I look at my old print now
and an old Ordnance Survey of his.
They both show a world I can barely believe.
A world that was marvellous, that was good.

The Missing Tablet

The fight against illicit trafficking in cultural goods requires the use of practical tools disseminating information, raising public awareness and preventing illegal exportation.
– EMERGENCY RED LIST OF IRAQI CULTURAL OBJECTS AT RISK

FIRST CATEGORY: WRITING. CLAY OR STONE TABLETS
Cultural Object 16180: Sumerian Tablet from Umma

Condition: lower corner broken, cracked middle; seal impressions
Inscriptions: obverse: administrative text, temple accounts
reverse: nature of text uncertain

The Amorite who knows no grain
Who knows no house nor town
The boor of the mountains
High as the height of cedars
Who digs up truffles
But does not bend his knees [to cultivate the land]
Who eats raw meat
Who is not buried after death

Three days' journey by boat
In the garments of cowherds
He made a black palace among those people
In the city of a million soldiers
Riches in royal measure
Remain with him there

Iceberg

Because the sky was full, attention fell
to hollowing a place below: slow scooping and sump pumps.
All that earth piled to a horrible mound of glistening
outside our window. This did not bode well, I thought.

Of course, the city has always been cool.
We'd just slipped to this pocket of warmth – a flat
not flat of bowed walls, skew floor holding us apologetically,
reminding how uncertainly we live. And the heat soon abandoned us.

What is it made of? I'd ask. No one knows
but rumours say it gorges on swimming pools and ballrooms, subsuming yoga studios,
bowling alleys, car carousels – whatever it can mass, freeze, hoard.
You admit you'd always fancied a cigar parlour.

Under tyres and railings, tarmac and shifting stone,
the cavity fills with an energy insalubrious. Cold-blooded kraken – it's growing,
I know it. You shrug, breakfasting on burnt toast. And it's useless to question
the men outside, messengers of the grim power.

Another night awake on my own, I hear it humming, making the rats
run. Sewers beneath are laced in crystal, streets sink and the groundwater
worries, collecting itself heavily. We'd claimed this spot

together, so what of our foundations? The bed now a raft
while a lunatic sucks at the glass, threatening soft and silver. Soon
all traces will drift.

Cave

is
    no thing
    but light
          play
articulating stone
    the strike & pick
strung
between
    no thing
    but air
pressed in each rift
    lift & drop
          handling
as the world
          tilts

[tide turn]

surfaces
    shiver
    in conversation
& masses
          dissolve to
    no thing
    but water
          clear
    bled from the
          bay's arm

driftwood
          adds to
    the vocabulary
    of forms
for what else
          does
    the soundless
base speak
          in the dark
          dark

White Line Fever, or Highway Hypnosis

The sun sets at the end of the road.
Temperature barely shifts, though—
pitch-hot, warmth in the ears,
and eyes smart wet and salt.

A white line marks the middle of the road
lying—winding shoelace—along
150 miles of continual road.
The hours follow, passing slow.

Roadside shadows play puppetry,
hunkered bushes and skittering rocks.
Surface printed scale-like—
what do you hear? The road is soft.

Head torch bores light into the road
and I'm stepping it, just—
                              when the sky
        keels
its giant lung
                    grey
                        juddering
                                slides—
        till it's melting itself
                    no time
                                to swim
                this salt road
feet steering
                    shoe boats
        the white
curls—
                        peeling tentacle
        bares
                    lone and binding
                so
the road
                                splits—
        I can't shake it
knowing that if
                    I fell
                        were to lie cool
        upon this broad line of line—
I would after all be held.

Orange County, CA

the drought's come

brush & scrub
hot orange blanched
to greys & browns
petrified dry wood
branch spikes skeletal
in a wilderness graveyard
tinder stacks | chucked
litter wait for no one

the drought's come

continuing on
the carpool diamond lane
others clogged with singles one
by one we crawl to the city
heart | BEEP of the toll
as the pumpjacks flare
out the glass & oldies
play on K-Earth 101

the drought's come

sun stains seats
gold with skin-ripping
heat but air con numbs
in shadow sweet white
corn from Mexico sold
—here the fruit once hung!
bulbs cheap all year
& plump | gone

the drought's come

horizon of roofs
& swimming pools
headlines spell doom
bear attack | coyote hunt
dusty streambed strewn
our daily extinctions
Saddleback Mountain
broods | feel it—

the drought's come

From Devín Castle

two weeks after my birth   we did meet
Nina from *ninati* meaning dream   here
the tower stands at the rivers' confluence
the Morava meets the Danube   the frontier
the marches   from *deva* meaning maiden
I have your eyes   lovesick girls jumped
to their deaths   a ruin   water meets water
it is a survivor   the curtain fell   a matter
of life   yes   it is also a fortress   we watch
from the border   *that* belongs to *those*
featured on coins   when you left this place
from *doiv* meaning light   to remember
we write it   the alphabet of the saints
she was given an even number of flowers
heads bow   we passed white turbines
cornfields   crushed gold   light on water
from *div* meaning evil spirit   the maiden
how you look like her!   I think it true
on the saint's day   when the town whirls
but where is the tower   it was on a map
placed stones   I really can't remember
still sunflowers   you   a curtain through
the window   bells and *babka*   meaning
grandmother   all over   red and white
in the mayor's square   across the river
one synagogue stands   when the country
split   what does it mean   not from that
shore   I take off my shoes and   jump

Between Spaces

the built, not-built and inbetween | lost, or what never
was | oasis of ornament | off-the-scale with a racked-up bill
| *where the moon king rides ever under moonlight* | banking
crisis | a scarcity of funds | debt | drought | doubt
| disputed territories | political indelicacies | the death of
the architect | temporarily 'put on hold' | *my client is
not in a hurry* | high stress | pressure points | the
movement of what should never move | collapsing
mathematics | where flights of fancy meet design flaws |
its parts ballooned like sugar loaves! | unimaginable | it
takes the breath away | [pause] | youthful optimism | or
else, illogic | hurricanes | flooding | subsidence | war
| plague-pit | test-site | set-back | excavated skulls |
exuberant graffiti on a concrete shell | informal
communities | differences of opinion | disrepair | a
shake of hands | change of hands | sleight of hands |
under the canopy of heaven | no where | morning breaks

LETTERS
FAIR

Small Talk

My life is a reducing act: all of it.
The less that is known, the more
assuredly held the convictions.
Each conversation, a paraphrase.
We meet to summarise the time
between meetings; chit-chat.
Stop thinking, start talking!
What's your mantra? Shut up.
Moot intention. Polished surface.
A voice sounds phony if inconsistent
or entirely consistent (just saying).
It's easier to cut & paste   cut & paste
Select an automatic response. Tweet.
Say I never mean what I say I mean what-
ever. Substitute with pronouns:
you/I/who will take my place.
Wordlessness is not the same as silence
for crying out loud doesn't mean I'm said.

And So Inveigled

It began so quietly and darkly, ~~only~~ a softness to the shadow that soothed, not menaced. ~~And here~~ I was ~~here~~ lulled into the talk, ~~and~~ opening an ~~the~~ eye to the ~~inner secrecies and~~ layered ~~desires~~ histories ~~I'd been~~ balancing in the heart. Gentle urging, ~~you press All we can hope for~~ at a time ~~of~~ absent of earthshine and so inveigled, I sang and ~~spread slipping~~ the message, ~~as as~~ sure as wildfire, ~~but blackest~~ here it ~~flows fingernail tears open spreading wild through night how it appears~~ cut ~~splits~~ like a fingernails ~~ragging~~ raging into the blue, and spreading, how ~~does~~ it has appeared on ~~I can only~~ this ~~fateful~~ path, from first to ~~against the~~ last, yes ~~it is a graceless account an~~ unspeakable I would think it unspeakable

A Voice Between Two Things

after W. S. Graham

world	spaces	
	imagined	gestures
through	empty	
	significant	shapes
the sea	as	
	the sea	spinning
visual	disturbances	
	my	other
side of	language	
	invisible	to you
the construct	a silence	
	calligraphic	dream
drawing	thing	
	made	abstract
sky-trekking	new	
	uncommon	words
time or	oneself	
	or	how alone
one is	released	
	into the	human

# of consequence

#follow

a sick man's dreams
idle fancies

dolphin in
the woods

twin babies
sitting in
tin buckets

taking liberties

for whatever they are
works of humankind will pass away

#mutability

recent stories

right here
right now

closed eyes
held pose

packaging
for exported ceramics

soft recycled
materials

free delivery
on orders
above £—

#like

it gives pleasure to look

rainbow garnish
aubergine
ugh, coriander

swimwear
to suit
every body

filtered vista
wish you
were here

#YOLO

whimsical
of the floating world

hot pink blue
—amaryllis?
budding gold

#engagement

teaching manuals

promote
the act of copying

he put a
ring on it

#tag

contribution
of players

placards
scrape
skyline

#RT

by repeating the past
you end with an unknown image

underlined
book extract
vintage cover

41

fiction becomes a kind of truth
art at one with life

#optimisation

elements of falsity
improve

inkwell lark
moon rise

framed
frame

revelation

me

and the mysteries

cryptic
cliché
caption

#click

take everything in the universe
as subject matter

highlights

see url
link in bio
not irl

treasured and flawed
little things
all

of consequence

#follow

Killing the Darlings

You know why you're here
This isn't a game

When the toast is made
You're toast

A denouement
Requires accomplices

And kissed girls cry
While the oil spits

Time ticks
From the lost timer

Somebody's thrown in the towel
I wring my hands

For all rules
Must be obeyed

They insist
You butcher the rest

anon.

the work speaks

                 for itself

whoever may read

        pray for who wrote

unknown craftsman

         coat of darkness

finding no name

          to be called

who is calling

       what do you look for

glaring mark

          naked truth

the poet as poet

        has no identity

I'm nobody

          who are you

three fingers write

     the whole body labours

hating an author

        that's all author

and who was she

           tell us

a sailor

   rescued from savage waves

mysteries

     none can understand

what looked as if

     it would last forever

the last line

      a timely harbour

laying down the pen

      have a happy heart

god

       help my hands

amen

          – anon.

The Bookworm

devours words
how wondrous
the reverse
of crafting verse
this little grub
wholly swallows up
someone's song
what should exit
the mouth
not enter it
a thief in darkness
of ignorance
chewing up such
rich rumination
a book's skeleton
its strong binding
the irony is
this greedy insect
a guest who
steals the silver
will never be
one jot the wiser
having ingested
the jottings

The Con

By the time I learned
    Long gone
What I hadn't known
    Loose coin
The penny dropped
    Day dawned
I'd come around
    Seed sown
And cottoned on
    Bed made
The table laid
    Too late
All trust dissolved
    Hand dealt
But who to blame
    Dice thrown
The trick is played
    Undone

THE PLOT

Compass Rose

N

left of the rising sun
winter winds wake and
on my garden blow old
air phlegmatic boreas
aquilo seven oxen at
the plough bearded
man an arctic night

W

autumn vintage as   towards   sunrise
break to full flow   of water the liver
quietening earth spl   ods sanguine eurus
zephyrus favonius   in the morning
breezes fructifying   er turns oriental
setting furthest from   bluster unhealthful
lost or destroyed po   levante and hope

E

dessicated in late summer
direction of midday
cross right hand head
downward hot breath
with mighty roaring
black thick tempests
sweet sirius and crave

S

EAST

flowering spring wind towards sunrise slow without fail infancy
of water the liver moist warm green woods sanguine eurus altair
becoming light in the morning shining aurora prayer turns oriental
horizons beginnings of bluster unhealthful keep mild about right
levante and hope

In the beginning, we tended to consistency: identical plots, work patterns, nourishing the seeds we'd been given. But each developed at its own rate – floundering, flourishing – and, inevitably, the weeds crept in. There were methods of management, but such persistence was tiring. Only now do I admit, but I admired their decadence, heedless and self-assured. Green and eager, night-time was their time, the better unwatched; we'd wake to a glory riot. No single moment, but we were certainly growing apart – that is to say, sought our own paths, against or in reaction to, desperate for new. The elders became obsolete, moral codes for setting aside. Mine at first didn't thrive, resisting adornment. Things roached in thickets, a gradual burgeoning until – dramatic – the boundaries no longer held, overrun in surge, as something beckoned, insisted, and – the gate is opening.

In the dream I was trying to reckon
the rings of a sliced trunk
but kept losing count.

I saw in the hollow an old face.
Some god?
No one speaks its name.

cave, cave
beware, beware

It shelters in heartwood
and the tree is living.

SOUTH

yellow harvest sun afternoon bile and fire gallbladder choleric
notus auster destroyer of crops bringer of storms fecund labyrinth
desiccated in late summer direction of midday cross right hand head
downward hot breath with mighty roaring black thick tempests
sweet sirius and crave

The garden is becoming, loud with life. Outlines span with the hours, spilling crescents, while round buds burst to light held by verticals long and true. Each day I aim to trim and shape: fingertips sweep, weed the unwanted. Reap, repeat; I am as I do. The garden reveals its gardener. All forms here suggested – relation, balance, subtle contrast – promise what will emerge, blazing joy [something wraps like hair] while guesswork grows to faith. Come now, consider; this means that. Amazement [alarm] to sense what hatches within the loaded trellises – must all be wrung out, destroyed? Taking steps [nor map nor code]: as one path lightens, the other goes up in smoke. It feels safer in solitude. Most never dare to unlatch the gate, for to enter may be to inter [blind alley, wrong turn] – and the consequences released.

Bowed figures come with offerings
to press in the neat bed rows.

And under our feet, what grows?

WEST

autumn vintage as roses when warm blows break to full flower
closing adulthood quietening earth spleen dry and melancholic
zephyrus favonius light early breezes fructifying cave evening vesper
setting furthest from altar gloomy rough be lost or destroyed ponente
and seek fortune

[within]

—out of the garden we are wrenched thrust we the lost
without warning just drums and the drones such force
invisible drove all the trespasses strapped to our temples
emblazoned insignia marked now spat up and hands
dusted of gone from the resting place cradles and nests
all earthy hollows we glutted for years so much there to
satisfy yes slipped up undone and out out of the garden
rid and good riddance shunned as the weak and the rotten
loose and the frail succumbed all weeded it's done but
what's lost the plot thickens leaving no shade the sun falls
and all in the night at what cost we prey out of home our
habitat hounded of hope we out—

ᚦᚱᚾ

_____ for remembrance
_____ for curing wounds
_____ against sorcery in the graveyard
_____ for disease of the head
_____ to ease childbirth
_____ to open locks
_____ as inheritance
_____ for raising the dead

NORTH

left of the rising sun winter winds wake and on my garden blow
old air phlegmatic boreas aquilo seven oxen at the plough bearded
man an arctic night belonging to the lower world sacrifices too far
or clever a little stronger bringer of cold weather tramontane
and disbelief

Say a Peacock is a peacock, the Toad a toad. Let the Goat
be, release the Snake. A Pig does what it does, the Lion
itself, a Snail is already complete. All seems [un]natural.
Three dead kings offer hands, make of themselves a mirror
– who can forget. Placed between pit and throne, I adjust
the coordinates. And the ladder of knowledge? Secrets
have been promised in the workings of earth – viridity's
virtue. Let each do according to nature: in correspondence,
sympathy. For love may conquer all. May all be happy at
heart, that place of quiet carried in the breast. There is a
heaven in meditation, freedom in reverie – what things
are, what things could be – trusting the sun to rise and
winds to wake. The plot ensnares, inspires.

𝍖

haste to invest	time is short
much provided	most unearned
the weight of debt	a soul's expense
vanitas	ambition's check
dear artifice	daily bread
wanting	wealth
bound to bury	plots are full
the self	is its own pledge
a hand gives	lesson learned

MYSTIC ART

The Cosmic Egg

after Hildegard von Bingen

stars
the shade of
I saw all this and
why are you hiding
but she is book-learned
the voice of the unheard melody
the last shall be first and the first shall be last
there was a dark fire of such great horror that I
heavens opened and a blinding light of exceptional
again I heard the voice speaking to me from heaven
brilliance flowed throughout my entire brain and
could not look at it whose force shook the whole
for many may be called but few are chosen
to utter an unknown language
and she knows letters
gold in the mud
refused to write
living light
or eyes

---

lines to be read from top to bottom alternately

Charm'd: the Opiate Rod

water witching
the locked ground

lightning
spear cast broadly

napier's bones
in a wrecked world

from steep air angled
saltire cross

arcadian pipe
stones spiced red

rare fruit
in armour crowned

a house falls to the sea
reck this

the staff is steady
spawning

when it connects—
conducts

Hunter's Moon, or the Werewulf

Skin on the ash tree
Fur in the wound
A reddening
The dart hits true

Girdle of monkshood
A breaking wheel
Harvest's quick fellow
Outcast at dusk

Fireworks

I would not think to touch the sky with two arms
– SAPPHO, TR. ANNE CARSON

Dogs are shouting.
As though the air were shot
through, such thudding.

Glitter staggers in sequence,
bright birds shocked from trees
greet with colour, soar farewells.

The sky is requisitioned.
Flung fire, the jewels
and feathers of artifice.

I must witness the spectacle,
cannot understand its works.
(wild blazes elsewhere)

Glory undoes the night
briefly. Pageantry of powder,
chemical masque.

To touch the sky
writing the darkness out, out –
arms reach.

ATLAS

A

As A

An ariA

ApologiA

Accept my pleA

As a lingua ignotA

Ah, galactic glossolaliA

Above I watch in panoramA

Adopt a burden through each erA

Arches all require almighty staminA

Afflicted by insomnia, regular melancholiA

Acute hypothermia or other such phenomenA

Although rewarded, too, by circadian cornucopiA

Audience to wild exuberance of astral extravaganzA

Astonished by the cosmic dance, night-time's euphoriA

And yet afflicted, continually, by one unanswered enigmA

Anyone – is anyone out there? Alone, I compose this fantasiA

Arms unfold their embrace and I lower just once to kiss the vistA

As if I were the sun escaping its mantle of dusk, settling into the seA

Soaring Flight

The sea is mood

    it edges the vision
                    field
    with its blue
      not blue
            so how will I be held

Greenscape
      mass
             pouring

the coast I gasp
             entangled in
     air

thrusts
      & backing
      wind

Up here
      I'm bucked

drift hitting
sky-blocks

                Shift
      to the stall
                turn
red route home

      thinned
            now

nosing
      for

        call it

      loss

True Artifice

Entrancing it is to wander, harmony in blue and gold.
Golden ornament – like the literary game, symbols of love,
love of freedom – dislodges minds, unmakes many worlds.
Worlds created from words. We have talked long enough,
naive reflections. To marvel is the beginning of knowledge;
knowledge (an opportunity for us) increases unreality.
Unrealisable ideals may yet make change imaginable.
Imagined alternatives, out of chaos, frame a thing of beauty.
Beauty is difficult, unlike the telling of beautiful untrue things,
things that don't exist: a good island, mystery's holy guardian,
garden of bright images, our perfection, man-made dream,
dreams like a diadem. For a few bright moments to be reborn,
resolutely artificial, enigmatical, through art. To what end?
End up as a book or work – neither begins nor ends; pretend.

Blessing

I wish you owl eyes
a violin at the heart
hair of candlelight
that sister smoke
three running wheels
the length of spine
bridge of knuckles
waving flamingos
and a lioness glare
two ankle prisms
in a dish of feathers
songbirds stringing
from the armpits
scales and thorns
speech of ladders
time a skipping egg
mouth filled with rain
groin's herb of grace
poise of the aurochs
an open chest
key in the palm
gallop to morning

Notes

A THING MADE

Poetry . . . is an 'artifact' – I mean, it is a thing made.
– GILBERT MURRAY, *CLASSICAL TRADITION IN POETRY*

'Work Study': borrows its setting from the studio of artist Caroline Walker (b.1982).

'Annunciation': after *The Annunciation* by Federico Barocci (*c.*1585).

'The Painting of the Queen': after *Queen Elizabeth I* by unknown English artist (*c.*1588).

'Wood Cut': after *Dracole wyade* (Vlad III 'the Impaler') by Markus Ayrer (1499) and written for 'The A to Z of Villainy' event at the Betsey Trotwood, London (2018).

'Waxworks': borrows its setting from Madame Tussauds.

'Portrait in Hex': the hex codes refer to 'seashell', 'shadow blue', 'pale chestnut' and 'Aztec gold'.

BASELESS FABRIC

And, like the baseless fabric of this vision,
The cloud-capped towers, the gorgeous palaces,
The solemn temples, the great globe itself,
Yea, all which it inherit, shall dissolve.
– SHAKESPEARE, *A MIDSUMMER NIGHT'S DREAM*

'The Mapmaker's Daughter': after the *Hereford Mappa Mundi* (*c.*1300).

'The Missing Tablet': developed from a collaboration with John Clegg for the Poetry School Camarade (2016).

'Cave': after *Sculpture with Colour (Deep Blue and Red) [6]* by Barbara Hepworth (1940).

'Between Spaces': after La Sagrada Família, the palaces of Ludwig II of Bavaria and various architects' models at the Victoria & Albert Museum.

LETTERS FAIR

But he that learns these Letters fair, shall have a Coach to take the Air.
– ANDREW TUER, *THE ROYAL BATTLEDORE*

'And So Inveigled': developed from a poetic interview with Aaron Kent (2017).

'A Voice Between Two Things': includes some of W. S. Graham's own words, discovered in his letters, poems and notebooks.

'of consequence': after the *Hokusai Manga* (Thames & Hudson, 2018) and Horace's 'On the Art of Poetry' in *Classical Literary Criticism* (Penguin Classics, 1978).

'anon.': after various Old English manuscript marginalia, and other writings related to authorship and nobodies.

'The Bookworm': a version of 'Riddle 47' from the *Exeter Book* (*c.*960–990).

THE PLOT

'West': after *Minerva Expelling the Vices from the Garden of Virtue* by Andrea Mantegna (1502).

MYSTIC ART

Whence did the wondrous mystic art arise,
Of painting speech, and speaking to the eyes?
That we, by tracing magic lines, are taught
How to embody, and to colour thought?
– WILLIAM MASSEY, *THE ORIGIN AND PROGRESS OF LETTERS*

'The Cosmic Egg': after *Hildegard of Bingen: The Woman of Her Age* by Fiona Maddocks (Faber & Faber, 2001).

'Charm'd: the Opiate Rod': for Roddy Lumsden (1966–2020).

'Hunter's Moon, or the Werewulf': developed from a poetic interview with Aaron Kent (2017).

'ATLAS': after *The Dance* by Nancy Spero (1993).

'Soaring Flight': after *Soaring Flight* by Peter Lanyon (1960).

'True Artifice': a cento sonnet made of lines from the following works: Veronica Forrest-Thomson, *Poetic Artifice* (Shearsman Books, 2016); E. H. Gombrich, *Art and Illusion* (Princeton University Press, 1969); J. K. Huysmans, *Against Nature*, tr. Robert Baldick (Penguin Classics, 1966); Ursula K. Le Guin, 'A War Without End', in *Utopia* (Verso, 2016); John Livingston Lowes, *The Road to Xanadu* (Constable, 1970); Stéphane Mallarmé, *The Book*, tr. Sylvia Gorelick (Exact Change, 2018) and 'Les Fenêtres', in *Collected Poems and Other Verse*, tr. E. H. and A. M. Blackmore (Oxford University Press, 2006); Thomas More, *Utopia* (Verso, 2016); James McNeill Whistler, *Harmony in Blue and Gold: The Peacock Room* (1877); Oscar Wilde, *The Decay of Lying: And Other Essays* (Penguin Classics, 2010); W. B. Yeats, 'Sailing to Byzantium' and 'The Statues', in *The Collected Poems of W. B. Yeats* (Wordsworth Editions, 2000).

'Blessing': after Leonora Carrington and for Leonora Sheldon.

Acknowledgements

Thank you to the editors of the following publications, where some of these poems – or versions of them – have appeared:

> *berlin lit*; *The Caught Habits of Language* (Donut Press, 2018); *Journal of Italian Translation* (poems tr. Leonardo Guzzo); *The Kindling Journal*; *Magma*; *Poetic Interviews* (Broken Sleep Books, 2019); *Poetry Review*; PROTOTYPE; *Snow lit rev*; *The White Review*.

There are many who have influenced or supported my writing. I give deeply appreciative thanks to:

> foundational inspirational figures: Ariane Jurriaanse, Amanda Silk, Helen Barr, Ariane Koek and Christopher Ricks

> formative places and spaces: the Beaufort Society; the Oxford University Poetry Society; *Oxford Poetry*; Roddy Lumsden and the Wednesday Group; *Poetry Review* and the Poetry School; Royal Holloway, University of London and its Spice Girls; and the University of Roehampton

> cherished former colleagues: Stephen Stuart-Smith, Isabel Brittain and the Enitharmon family

> all the talented employees and poets at Faber, from whom I learn every day, and Eleanor Crow for her fine eye

> the king of experiment and generosity: Steve Fowler

> a magnanimous poetry mentor who made and makes so much happen, for me and for so many: Fiona Sampson

> an expert surveyor of paper houses, and guiding light: Matthew Hollis

> the talented team at Prototype and assisting freelancers: including Rory Cook, design wizard Magnus Hearn of Studio Foss, proofreader Aimee Selby and author photographer Robin Silas

> my marvellous editor, whose belief builds and integrity inspires: Jess Chandler

> lifelong supporters of creativity and the imagination: Juliet Singer, Marc Miller and Wolfgang Kaiser

> my dear, loyal friends: who enrich and encourage, endlessly

> my beloved families: the Tilleses, the Etchegarays, the McCrickerds and Mabel

> the core and the heart: my parents and Amelia, who made me

> my babies: Audley, Juniper and the newest soon-to-be

> my life partner, who enables all things and (beyond words): Ryan.

About the Author

Lavinia Singer is the author of the pamphlet *Ornaments: a handbook* (If a Leaf Falls/Glyph Press, 2020) and co-editor of *Try To Be Better* (Prototype, 2019), a creative-critical engagement with the work of W. S. Graham. *Artifice* is her first full collection of poetry.

About Prototype

poetry / prose / interdisciplinary projects / anthologies

Creating new possibilities in the publishing of fiction and poetry through a flexible, interdisciplinary approach and the production of unique and beautiful books.

Prototype is an independent publisher working across genres and disciplines, committed to discovering and sharing work that exists outside the mainstream.

Each publication is unique in its form and presentation, and the aesthetic of each object is considered critical to its production.

Prototype strives to increase audiences for experimental writing, as the home for writers and artists whose work requires a creative vision not offered by mainstream literary publishers.

In its current, evolving form, Prototype consists of 4 strands of publications:

(type 1 — poetry)
(type 2 — prose)
(type 3 — interdisciplinary projects)
(type 4 — anthologies) including an annual anthology of new work, *PROTOTYPE.*

Artifice by Lavinia Singer
Published by Prototype in 2023

The right of Lavinia Singer to be identified as author of this work has been asserted in accordance with Section 77 of the UK Copyright, Designs and Patents Act 1988.

Design by Studio Foss
Typeset in Tiempos Text

Printed in the UK by TJ Books Ltd

ISBN 978-1-913513-35-1

( ) (   )
 p   prototype

(type 1 – poetry)
www.prototypepublishing.co.uk
@prototypepubs

Prototype Publishing
71 Oriel Road
London E9 5SG
UK

ISBN 978-1-913513-35-1

9 781913 513351 >